The Horse and Her Girl

A Rocky Ride to Womanhood

Memoir by

FIONA MCILROY

This is a work of nonfiction.

Ordering Information:

Prime Seven Media
518 Landmann St.
Tomah City, WI 54660

Printed in the United States of America

Trust is a Prerequisite for Happiness

In Bhutan and Switzerland, trust is highly valued. Studies have found that trust—more than income or even health—is the most significant factor in determining our happiness.

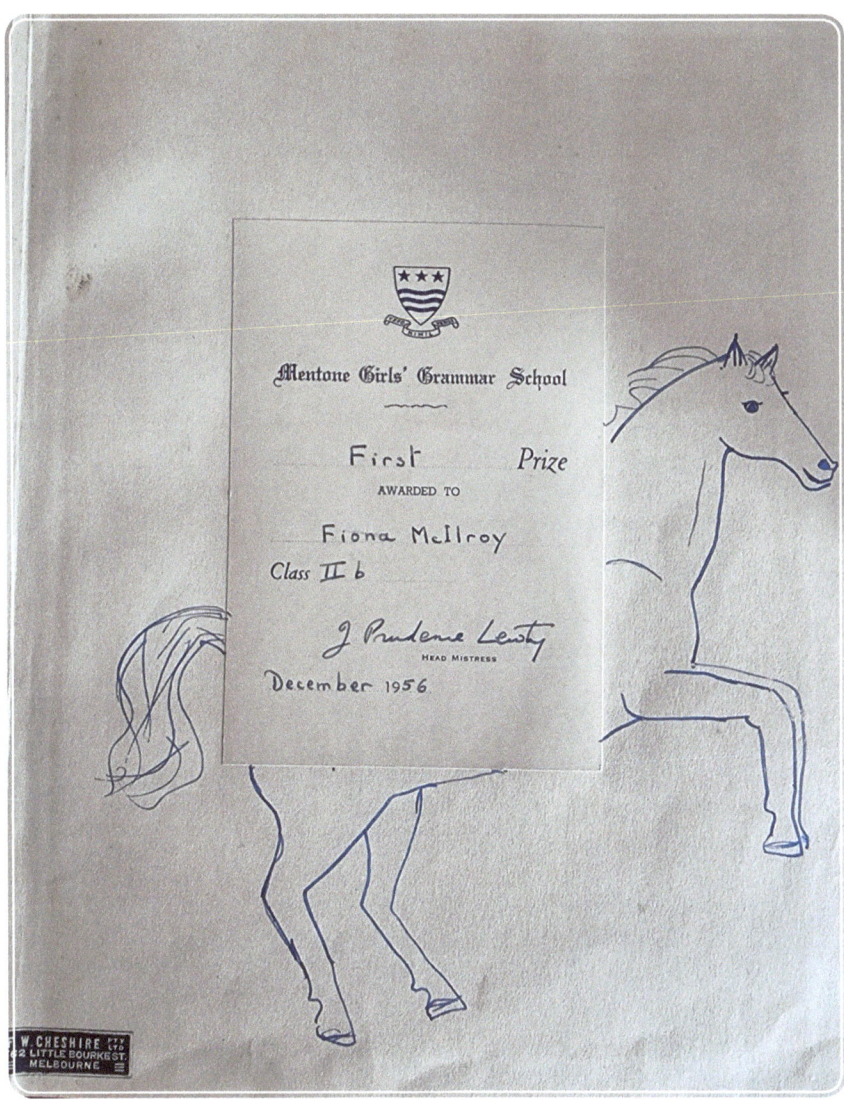

Table of Contents

～ 1 ～

How did my love of horses begin

*W*hat is it that is magic about the movement on horseback? For me, it overtakes the movement in a car, on a bike, on a train, a plane, a boat in the sense of union, of rhythmic interaction and even harmony between two conscious beings. The rhythm shifts from a careful steady walk to a fluid rocking side to side canter. A Bach cantata. A calm chorale.

In the moment

time is elastic
when on horseback
across the tableland

each milestone
a monument
in the memory

a moment in space
suspended with
the rider
beginning to end

hooves tapping
on the tarmac
in minuets

no movement
of minutes
just dawn to dusk

Riding bareback on a steady, gentle-natured pony willing to go from walk to canter is a delight. Flying on a rocking chair is as close to the feeling I can convey. After the ride, warm slide off her back, stroke her neck, and touch the softest velvet on earth just above her flared nostrils. Communion. No need to go to the chapel today.

Communion

no need to go to the chapel
today
take the closest path
to communion
stroke the velvet
above the nostrils
of the mare
then breathe-
in unison

While riding along rocky trails with amazing alpine views on either side, I realized that unlike walking, riding a reliable horse meant I could relax and look at the vista around me. Riding along the Bowen range staring into pastiche snow gum and manna gum woodland,

and down into the valley where kangaroos and emus graze peacefully. wallabies, wombats and echidnas cross our path with hardly a glance. Somehow the quiet mare gave them no reason to scuttle off. Lizards, snakes and skinks also tended to stop in their tracks and wait for us to pass.

~ 2 ~

Why trust a horse ?

*O*ver my accident-filled life, I had relatively minor falls from a horse. A common refrain from friends was that a life on horseback is dangerous. Over a span of 40 years on horseback, I can only say that car accidents, house accidents or falls while walking were my downfall. Horses were as safe as houses …. no, safer.

This story follows the rocky ride of a girl to womanhood that could have stopped her in her tracks, but in reality gave her courage to keep reaching, hoping, giving and receiving love. Derek, the riding instructor would tell me: 'Hold onto the reins, but be gentle with the horse's mouth. Otherwise it will harden and not respond to your directions.'

Could this be a metaphor for keeping an open heart even when it has been broken time and time again? For some reason, I decided to be whole-hearted rather than shut down the capacity to trust. My journey with horses took me through deep chasms and high peaks, and taught me to accept death and live life with an open heart. An incurable optimist, you say? A Pollyanna, said my dad, brother and husband- (all believers in Murphy's Law. 'What can go wrong will go wrong')…and: "don't expect it to happen. Fate will step in"…On this last point Pollyanna agrees with Murphy. I have made have even made overheads for my life balance workshops: *Hope, but don't expect an event to go well.*

I feel that one can remain open and vulnerable to experience, otherwise life will brush past and never leave an indelible mark, whether deeply challenging or life-affirming. As I grew up I asked questions that related to meaning. I delved into spiritual realms that my parents were unwilling to explore. They had moved away from their Christian education to evidence based theory. Perhaps this is the origin of my love of poetry, where intuition is combines with ideas, and dreams are woven into everyday experience in a search for meaning.

I was moved to draw horses, write poetry and stories from the age of five, as soon as I had stopped writing backwards. Being a left-hander, I later found out, was a trait more common in those whose right brain was dominant, and this was linked to such aberrations as writing backwards and being intuitive, or 'spontaneous' or as my scientist father, (and later my husband) would say.

Singing stones

each of us owns
a dry creek-bed
crying out
for its singing stones

take out the stitches
from old scar tissue
covering up
some painful issue

unleash the tears
long locked inside
roll off the rock
let go the pride

our psychic springs
will not run dry
if we choose to live
before we die

neuronal pathways
ingrown, inbred
seal our hearts off
from our head

mental mantras
now stone-dead
tell us to act on
what others have said

each of us owns
a dry creek-bed
crying out
for its singing stones

I was fascinated to learn that recently the inhabitants of mountain regions ie Bhutan and Switzerland have globally high levels of happiness- based on valuing trust, rather than income or security.

On reflection, my life has been a pursuit of trust. Even though trust has been repeatedly broken and challenged in my close relationships and life circumstances. I have restored my capacity for trust. It is the basis for love and life.

Is it a Pollyanna miasma- a childish illusion, (as my brothers have said) or a sign of immature wishful thinking? Or is it the choice of a poet, a woman who likes to wonder, a wanderer, a lover of peak experience, a left-hander with left and right hemispheres holding hands, a mystified awe-struck devotee of life in all its exquisite but unexpected rifts and gifts? Fate, fear or fickle friends or lovers can do their utmost damage but I am born to love. I commit to loving till my final breath.

Oratorio at Bowen Creek

now I know what to do
when my heart is ruffled
torn or battered in a storm

now I know where to go
when my mind is baffled
by the pressure to perform

just walk a bit more slow
to where sound is muffled
soft carpet of starry lawn

from the log- look below
where strobe lights dapple
the granite rock form

all shades of green glow
from pomaderris to apple
from moss to tree fern

the thrill of each arpeggio
as thrush and gang-gang grapple
with tree creeper and scrub wren

the solo gong of oriole
against the rise and free fall
of speckled warbler or wattlebird

hours pass by in liquid flow
as shimmering pebbles ripple
bathing the eye in light and shade

on the way back to the cabin
you can be royally entertained
by the king of mimics-lyrebird

the Marcel Marceau des oiseaux
dancer, romancer, ventriloquist
and studio artist superb

now I know where to go
to the source of all I seek
the birth of the Word, the babble
of Bowen Creek

the oratorio improvised each
dawn and dusk just for us-
surround -sound tones
from birds and singing stones

3

Trauma at age five

A serious incident of sexual abuse as a five year old girl cast a long shadow. I had played with my brothers and the neighbourhood kids every day in Foam Street in Parkdale, a suburb on the Port Philip Bay, Melbourne. In the early 1950s, no parental supervision was considered necessary. We played with goats, chooks at Molly's place across the road, on the nature strip, in the street with poison ball, in the vacant block with long grass and an old broken sulky.

This was where the 'play' often was, source of my fear of spiders and snakes, to be confronted by teasing, coaxing and touching games that led to pain and insertion of sticks and stones in my private parts. As it was older kids who lived a few houses away, I did not realise they were the abused becoming the abusers, threatening me with their dad's horsewhip if I did not let them do things to me. No one could hear or see what was taking place in the scrub- though right next to our blue weatherboard respectable home. The older kids held me down and planted sticks or stones in my vulva.

After one nasty incident, I recall sitting on the toilet in pain unable to go, but unwilling to tell my mum what had happened. I felt to blame for playing with the kids on the broken sulky in the overgrown grass.

The saga culminated in a hospital drama. I thought they were trying to kill me when they covered my mouth with chloroform, and I fought off the nurses till they called on help to pin me down. As a five year old I must have felt they were punishing me for being caught up in this vile game.

Surgery to remove the foreign objects meant recovery time, (blanked out) and of course my parents changed my school to ensure I did not have contact with the neighbour's kids. In hindsight more could have done to get to the source of the abuse- the father with the horsewhip. I wonder how those kids grew up, and whether other kids were abused by them. I must have felt very wrong and traumatised for weeks or months, as I recall walking alone every lunchtime around the quadrangle. Feeling like a cockroach or a coldsore- visible to everyone but unable to ask for help.

No doubt these incidents of sexual abuse at the hands of older children led to a sense of guilt, shame and timidity. If it had been an older man, perhaps I could have told my parents. Coupled with my natural shyness, sensitive nature and a lively imagination, I responded well to forming deep bonds with people and animals I could trust.

The stories I am relating in this memoir are snapshots of the more significant or indelible turns of event. For me, trust hinges on self-awareness and sensitivity to each other in relationship. Learning to trust a horse was a good confidence-builder. Lesson one: choose a horse that you can trust and can trust you.

4

Fairy, the first quiet pony

Every summer school holiday mum and dad drove the family (brothers Jim, Bob, and younger sister Fran) up to Armidale, to Dyamberin where we stayed with grandparents in the cottage with roses and vegie patch. After they passed away, we stayed with Uncle Brud. He bred horses for managing a large cattle and sheep property owned by the Wright family for a century. My love of horses started there, since luckily the uncle started me on a quiet pony Fairy. Soon I joined the cousins, uncle and aunt riding out for a day of drafting and droving herds into new pasture; even leaning to open a gate from horseback without getting on and off. Every chain on a gate had its own trick.

Judith Wright was my mum's elder cousin, and she had been mum's home school tutor for a year or two at Dyamberin. In adulthood Judith and mum became the black sheep of the conservative family, being seen as radical feminist and environmentalists. After mum was tutored by Judith Wright as a teenager, she got restless. Just before World War II broke out, she took off to study Social Work in Sydney. She broke the mould for her family, as did Judith. They remained close as the conservation and environmental challenges divided the wider community.

At times my stays with Wrights were deeply challenging and even lonely, when my parents travelled for up to six weeks overseas for dad's research projects. Each of my siblings stayed with a different family. Generous of them, but culture clashes were clear.

Feeling stupid and awkward not knowing how to set the table with two knives and forks, or how to say grace before eating, or how to put the bridle on properly.... I felt like a newbie in boarding school; only these other kids were cousins not schoolmates. Our parents were progressive university-educated adults who did not believe in ultra conservative rules.

Our family with four kids moved to a bush block with an acre, enough space for a horse paddock. I think my parents recognized my tendency to withdraw and become despondent as a child. They may have recalled the trauma in the background.

Fortunately for me, my mother and father were prepared to support my intense wish at the age of 12 to have a pony of my own. Only later did I fully realise the extent of the cost to them and my three siblings, as the pony enterprise was expensive in money and time. But I also appreciated the companionship and close bond formed with each of the horses I was blessed to know, love and lose. As well, the bond with the horse helped to develop a sense of self and heal wounds from betrayal of trust in the adult world. It was only later in my life that key traumatic incidents stood out in my personal journey, and how crucial the relationship with a special equine friend has been in restoring confidence and trust in the world.

∾ 5 ∾

Silver- a horse of my own

First there was Silver, a sensible, plain-looking gray gelding who taught me to ride in a reasonably relaxed fashion. He differed from many of the Pony Club ponies in his unflappable steady state, no shying, no biting or kicking. Sedate, Reliable. I never wanted to try my hand with the quixotic, temperamental, hot-blooded, quick-tempered and fast-paced ones. I felt safe with Silver, and trusted him.

We explored the bush at the back of our new suburb, jumping fallen logs and trying new paths. My friend and I also sometimes pulled out survey pegs as an act of rebellion against continuing development of the bush we so loved! Pony club on Saturdays, gymkhanas, ribbons and then, excitement! Silver and I were in a team to compete at the Royal Melbourne Show. However, a particularly untimely and unexpected incident changed all that for Silver and I.

One day, before I left for school, the man who agisted Silver on his land called to tell me Silver had colic and I had better call the vet. We did, and I decided to miss school and go up to see him. The horse was no longer silver-gray. He was black, caked with mud and blood. His eye was red and unseeing. He did not respond to my voice. I talked to him. I stroked his cold neck. He was standing but shaky. The man who had him agisted in his paddock kept telling me to go home and let the vet look after him. "When the vet gives him a shot, he'll be right as rain, he'll be a different horse tomorrow. It's no use you standing around moping."

I stayed stubbornly for an hour or more, trying to take on board how sick he was and how likely he was to die. His sunken eye told me he had given up. Walking home, I was very downhearted. Grappling with the fact of death of a loved one. Almost ready to accept Silver was past saving. Kept picturing his clouded eye and lack of response. Tried to do homework desultorily. Then the vet rang to say, "Bring a rug and a bucket of feed."

I raced downstairs to grab the things, heart soaring with relief and thudding against my disbelief. Having adjusted to the possibility of losing the beloved creature, I had a rush of hope- the vet had cured

Silver like a magician! I packed the rug and bucket of feed, and my mum got ready to drive me up. The phone rang again. It was the vet again, "I am afraid your horse has gone. I had to end his misery.

The scream that shot out of me was animal agony. I cried "No No" and ran around the living room, tearing at the curtains. My mum was scared and led me to my room, shouting at me to calm down. I banged my head on the desk, and for hours my father kept coming in to bring tea and comfort.

This experience had a huge impact on my nervous system. People reassuring me that things will get better makes me alarmed. If I sense a realistic danger, people trying to cheer me up by saying: "it will be all-right" makes me sick. If I feel my hope soaring, I quickly pull it back to a moderate level. High hopes are dangerous- a trigger for fear. Perversely, though, I continue to be a hopeful person, known among family and friends as a Pollyanna, seeing the glint of sunlight on the leaf after heartbreak as a sign of love returning.

A single diamond

A single diamond
dazzles me
a Banksia leaf
with a drop of dew
brings my eye to you

the arrow of hope
pierces through
fear to relief

morning sun
can relieve
an open heart

even one torn apart
like that ancient tree
by lightning
can shine again.

6

Marinka:
the second fatal loss

Seeing how devastated I was after the Silver tragedy, my parents asked me if I wanted to have another pony or just rely on riding at Pony club. This was kind of them. I asked Derek at the riding school to keep an eye out for a quiet but willing pony for me to stay in the saddle. (And bareback...). I tried a couple of ponies but the first one had a hard mouth, took the bit in his mouth. The next one shied at posts and trucks. I hung on a few months.

Derek told me about an unusually quiet 2 year-old pony, bay, gentle eye, responsive mouth and no kick or bite. It was unusual for a part thoroughbred (she must be an accidental foal, he reckoned) to be so placid. Stroking her gave me a sense of smooth aristocracy, silky sophistication. The only element of Marinka's presentation that saddened me was her neck had a dip instead of a curve- caused according to Derek, by poor nutrition as a foal. Possibly, he reckoned, she had been taken young from her racing mother as she was the result of an accidental affair with a pony...but since she was quiet, almost too quiet, and obedient; with a gentle eye and lovely head, I decided to try her.

By now, our dad had fenced an acre or two on our place. I kept her close to keep an eye on her. We bought hay and oats to feed her. She also kept our lawn mown. I recall riding Marinka around Mt Eliza in 1960, when as it was dirt roads, houses with large gardens and bushland. She seemed bulletproof, almost half asleep. Had to kick her to get her into a trot.

Then one day, a small terrier yapped at her heels. Suddenly she leaped into a canter, and started swerving side to side. I could barely stay on, and as soon as I could pull her up, I slid off. It was as if she had woken from a trance.

From that time on, any dog, bike, car braking or door slamming set her into a panic. Things escalated till I took her back to Derek, who said he would set her straight. He did his best, but when she returned to me, she was still spooked by many things. Once when we got to the top of our driveway, she reared suddenly and whacked my jaw. The result was two loose front teeth and one knocked out. After that, I was nervous. But to add to the challenge, Marinka's legs began to swell. The vet could not tell us what was wrong. It worsened till there was no chance of riding her.

Over about six weeks she got weaker and finally had to be put down by the vet. An unknown condition - did it stem from her unwanted birth? How did I deal with this? After the sudden tragedy with my beloved Silver, this was a double blow. I recall feeling as if fate was targeting me, that I did not deserve to be happy, that I was an unreliable horse owner. Why did I lose two ponies in a row? What did I do wrong?

Perhaps my parents secretly hoped I would give up on horses now. I did not want to own another pony while still at school. However, a close friend Sue had a pony that she had permission to graze at the lower school grounds. One day she and I dared to slip her out at lunch-time, and rode double bareback through the quiet Mentone streets, feeling like stars in a comic book we had written. Amazingly we returned without being caught, even by jealous schoolgirls. Sue was a horse aficionado who drew horses in charcoal with ease, and won many ribbons at shows. I must have felt like an amateur beside her. I was not the girl who was asked by the riding school instructor to ride the unruly bucking horses or the highly strung show - jumpers. I preferred the kind, reliable pony that responded to gentle touch; of course that ruled out both the excitable and the stubborn, bored kind of pony who has been over-used by beginners. Given how rare this good-natured kind of pony is, I was blessed to find true equine companions later in my life.

～ 7 ～

Restoring trust

*F*ortunately in my early 20s, the horse faith was restored. Somehow the need for a trusting relationship remained a priority. Somewhat surprising that I trusted that need. This trust extended to intimate relationships.

First romantic love at 15 was on a cruise ship to Arizona. Dad was going to a research post in Tempe Arizona to help with irrigation in an arid place, and we all went with him. I was in Year 11, quite prepared to be educated in a different setting. As it happened, high school in a conservative US State was a total shock. The level of conformity made my little Church Girls' Grammar seem progressive. At least there I recall having vigorous discussion about world peace.

My suitor kissed me on the deck under the stars, romanced and danced with me. This led me to believe in true love, leading to total devotion and ultimate commitment on return to Melbourne for Matric. Then after a year of weekly love letters from UK to Melbourne, my 21 year old romancer arrived in Australia, took me out to the Frankston pier, and said: I have met someone and we are engaged to be married. I was so shattered, I tried to jump in the deep waters of the bay. It was a week before my matriculation exams, and I recall almost being unable to sit the exams. Crying night and day- in shock. I had been a top English student but ended up only getting 2nd class Honours, and surprised to get First class Honours in French; a second language; less personally challenging perhaps..

But even now I recall thinking at the time how many songs stories and poems spoke of jealousy, betrayal and broken hearts. I told myself that I already had a broken heart, and could never love again without reservation. As many popular songs wailed, I should just stop myself from trusting love now. 'I will never love again..' Then I thought: would I want to go through life shielding myself from possible hurt and thereby denying myself the experience of passion and reciprocal love?...After thinking it through deeply I decided to keep an open heart and to reject my dad's Murphy 's law (whatever can go wrong will go wrong..) I wrote in my little book: *no matter what pain keeps company with love I will not abstain.*

The trajectory of my life has had multiple deep betrayals of trust. But a dedication to restore faith in serendipity, trust, love and happy outcomes has persisted. Close family and friends have sometimes been stumped at my determination to keep love alive. Perhaps for a shy, self-conscious girl it was a way to live as a warrior- to persist in living and loving whole-heartedly.

8

Growing alienation with city life

*F*or my Honours year in 1970, I changed campus from Melbourne to LaTrobe University. Now living in the Kinglake hills, most days I walked along the escarpment at dusk, looking down on the spread of the city of Melbourne. Often the air was clear where I stood, while a brown smear hovered over the urban centre, and rose to half way up the hill I stood on. This sight confirmed a sense of rising above the murky city air, and motivated me to live without the life I had become attached to while at University of Melbourne in Carlton- eg cappuccinos with friends, movies, bookshops to browse, trams and chance encounters.

I used to drive my Beetle bug VW down the winding road from Kinglake to Latrobe University for Honours English classes. One day, fate conspired to finish that chapter. I would arrive at tutorials with my long brown coat lined with burrs, or splashed with mud from a rural existence. When students read Wyatt or Dryden, Whitman or any ode to rural bliss they always asked me to read, and teased me about my "milkmaid attire".

The Honours English group protested about the lack of choice of units, and the lack of teaching time. I joined them, surprising my tutor who believed I was a top student, having topped the 2nd year at

University of Melbourne. However, since I had finished my Honours Thesis on Sylvia Plath and wanted to focus on living the good life in Kinglake growing vegetables, away from the rat race, I left the University. Academic pursuits now seemed ivory tower, lacking substance, removed from the earthly delights I had been tasting.

❧ 9 ❧

1970 - My first move 'back to the land'

I had been planning a 'back to the land' move with my paramour and two good friends. We found a forested place in the foothills, inland from Cobargo, South Coast of NSW, that felt beyond place and time. Six river cossings to get into the secluded river flat. We named it after the book by Kurt Vonnegut: Tralfamadore, where time is as elastic as space- since time stood still once you arrived there. It was a place to stay forever....Except when you ran out of flour, oats, or had to get the mail.

Things came unstuck after a few months. We all got infected sores from an unknown source, and my beloved left me. I went back to Kinglake nursing a broken heart. His bisexuality was known and accepted by me, so I never understood why he chose to hide relationships with my close women friends.

Too late
now you have come and gone
leaving a mist, almost rain
just a bit too late
for a good season

The next time I went to stay at Tralfamadore was on horseback after an epic five day ride from Cabanandra across the Monaro tablelands, and down the steep escarpment to the coast.

Katy's journey from mountain to the sea

With tapping hooves below
I took a journey thrumming
to my own blood's course

riding along the verge
of arterial roads
attracting lone horses
to a barbed wire fence
puncturing the soft
undulating breastbone
of the Monaro tableau
- meaning 'woman's breast'

we rounded shoulder after
shoulder of her cracked
eroded plains
giving flesh to five days
as full-bodied as any
I have known

through your gentle steady
steps, reins at the ready
never pulled
time has come and gone
in the wind-blown clouds
still here now

10

Finding Katy, the dream pony

While visiting some new friends on a farm in Kinglake, I spotted a lovely skewbald mare. I walked up to her, and patted her smooth solid neck. Her eye was the kindest eye I had ever seen in animal or person. This kindness was no cataract, no rose-tinted glasses, no lie. She continued to be the kindest natured beast on earth. This was my model, my article of faith. Katy became mine as soon as we met, and her canter from a walk was a dream while bareback riding. I could get on her without a stirrup to boost, though later I used a log, or just angled her back downhill from me. She was just 14.2 hands; a sturdy pony with a hint of Arab in her head and neck.

Katy became my anchor. She came with me when I moved to Cabanandra in 1972. Her kind spirit gave many children a dose of delight, and she delivered several quiet foals, with some pivotal moments to tell you later.

৯৯ 11 ৯৯

A lesson in boundary - setting

hen a dear friend Lyn found a teaching job at Yarra Junction High school, she told me there was a librarian position. I had completed my Arts degree in 1970 after dropping out of the Honours year to go bush. Lyn had found a little 2 bedroom cabin at the top of a hill close to the school. I was not to be parted from my pony, so hey presto! I brought Katy for transport to work! There was a yard next to the cabin, so she stayed over-night in the yard, and we were given permission to graze her near the school during the day. This was a dream .... well that part of it at least...as for the librarian job?

At first all went well. I had lots to learn about book classification etc just to find and keep books in their place. But the bigger lesson came in knowing how to set boundaries.

Teachers had a habit of sending disruptive students to the library. This was supposed to be a time out, a threat, removal from their peers, but it often worked in the opposite way; students developed outlaw status, enjoyed meeting other exiled students, and began a campaign to annoy the librarian, taking out books for no reason, reading loudly, even rocking shelves, playing hide and seek, making paper planes with newspapers, etc. I was unaware that I had the right to say 'no more thanks', so felt compelled to manage these outcasts, rebels, by getting them interested in a book or perhaps a small task. Occasionally I had worthwhile interactions with regular outcasts. But slowly the library became a place of refuge for the most emotionally challenged and challenging. When certain kids coincided, my methods of engagement were painfully inadequate.

Their behavior escalated, until one day I was in the midst of guerilla warfare, paper planes, rocking shelves, and a boy swinging on my swivel office chair. I lost it. They had struck my limit! I yelled loudly Stop! Come over here all of you.

Almost in disbelief, they crept over to stand in front of me, staring as if I had suffered a sudden transformation from doll to troll! I said :'I have been welcoming to you, right? I have been more than fair. Are you playing fair?' (heads slowly shaking)

'If you expect me to call in the big guns, send you to the principal for detention or caning, I am not going to give you the pleasure. I stand here to ask you to treat me with respect. To treat this library with respect. Your life with respect. Do you want to be thrown out of school? What then? I have never been treated so badly before. I refuse to roll over. Enough trying to be your friend. Until you start realizing being here is an opportunity to be cared about and listened to. I am leaving you now to clean up.'

I walked out of the library knowing other teachers had passed and paused to listen. Went straight to the staff room, stood staring out the window with my cup warming my hand, tears streaming down my face. When my favourite teacher Malcolm appeared by my side, I confessed what happened.

He said: 'Good thing too. They need to know you have limits.' I asked him how he had gained and kept the respect of the students, as he was highly regarded in working with troubled and challenging students.

After fifteen minutes, we walked together to the library and opened the door to a scene of complete makeover. Newspapers neatly folded, bookshelves tidy, students standing hands folded, smiling, rueful. 'Sorry Miss', they chorused. 'We won't do it again.'

After that, the offenders took advantage of my ready ear, and we became "Firm Friends", something not kosher at all for a teacher, but I figured OK for a librarian. Particularly now I realized I had the right to limit my numbers. The downside of the whole drama was that several teachers came in to shuffle and mumble beside me about not letting them see you are vulnerable, not to let them get to you etc. I realized my rise to fame in the staffroom was a fall from grace as a member of an adult community whose cover cannot be blown- the notion that we are impervious to attack and our defences are never breached. Never let them see you as a frail, vulnerable human being! I recognized that we were in a period between authoritarian and democratic education where nobody really knew how to handle discipline with boundary-pushing kids.

When the three-month contract came to an end, I think both the school and I were relieved. Even though an unexpected measure of success (to me) produced a treasured memory: several of the recalcitrants turning up with farewell and thank you cards on my last day!

A memory of jubilation is this: Lyn and I riding double on Katy down the track from our cabin on the hill to the school; the school bus with students whooping Indian style as they went past the painted pony with two riders they knew to be teachers riding bareback. What a sight! What a sound…hope they also remember the scene. Another reason the school may have been relieved to see me go….

12

Cabanandra,
a new beginning

*N*ow it was time to go to our new home in far East Gippsland 1972, Cabanandra. This meant taking her from Kinglake in a float. Katy showed a stubborn side that began with an absolute refusal to walk up the ramp to the horse float. After trying carrots, oats, blindfold, and then picking up her feet one by one while she was blindfolded (a last resort after ringing a vet for advice).

Eventually, the vet came to give her a tranquilliser as a last resort knowing we had a long arduous drive from Melbourne to Cabanandra. This includes tackling the Bonang highway from Orbost, which is said to have the most bends on any Victorian road! The journey was incredibly tense, and I had to stop many times to make sure she was awake and able to balance herself in the float. Never again, I swore to myself, would I put Katy in a float. As it turned out, that was an oath we kept …. another chapter in our adventures together that led to a very long ride.

Then came the beginning of life in a beautiful remote place in the foothills of the Snowy Mountains, where climate extremes kept us rocking. Cabanandra was my spiritual home.

we aim high
up here in the foothills
of the Snowy mountains

at night
our scalps prickle with stars

13

Riding up the Warm Corners gully, greeted by FIRE !!

It was certainly a dry first winter at our new Cabanandra home. We knew this was true not only because the frosts were severe and the milking cow needed constant feeding, but because our neighbours the Camerons claimed it was the worst they could recall. Spring came without any real rain. One morning I smelt smoke and noticed several plumes of smoke above Warm Corners gully. I decided to ride up the gully to check if it was the neighbours burning off - their annual fuel reduction effort. When we got to the top of the track where there are views of the Cobberas and Snowy mountains, I could see nothing but flames and smoke. Then Jim Cameron loomed out and he was looking worried. 'Get back home, girlie, and call the fire truck would ya?'

I needed no more encouragement. Katy and I took off down the gully, fearful of being pursued by the flames. When we got to the old house where Deb and the baby were waiting, I told her what we were asked to do. After calling the Tubbut firetruck, we took off with a few items, a pram, the baby and the horse. Looking back we wondered whether the fire would come down the gully. In our limited understanding bushfires usually travel uphill as heat rises. The neighbours drove their utes down in a rush. However, as we walked towards the mailbox across the Jingallalla, the fire leapt down the Warm Corners gully from ti-tree to tussock, almost reaching the house, then turned and swept along Garden Hill. We were stunned, and very relieved to have left.

When the firies arrived, they got out and squatted to watch the fire sweep across our hill. I still recall one man saying: she needs a good burn, hasn't had one since the last fire. I was mortified that they thought this was a healthy burn. It almost felt they were saying: good riddance to bad rubbish, its only bush. A couple of spot fires started from embers down on the river where we had friends camping. A tent went up in flames it turned out, but our friends were safe at the river. There we were, almost snuffed out or having our house burnt down by the neighbour's actions. Talk about trust on the edge!! We were utterly shaken, but still shaking our heads to come to terms with the near miss; not to mention the loss of our Garden Hill.

Somehow we returned and went to bed. I slept in the shed at the back of the old house. In the morning I awoke to a strange, muffled silence. Was this the sound of the morning after a bushfire? When I looked outside, flakes of snow were gently circling to the charred ground. Utterly unreal...I got up immediately and caught Katy. We found our way up the gully in a totally surreal scene, with charred and blackened vista pillowed with snow in hollows and on logs. In these times I did not have a camera at hand, so could only capture this chimera with my senses. Now it is hard to be believed, when trying to describe the speed of this weather extreme. We knew nothing about climate change at that time, but we thought: this is a sacred place we have found, where things happen that are beyond belief.....now I was a believer. Katy picked her way through the country where before she could not push past tea-tree and wattle. Now we could see far and wide. Would that I had snapped these scenes for posterity, as not many are able to believe that this really took place. Black magic.....turned white.

In the months at Cabanandra I was nursing a broken heart after my first foray into the pioneering back to the land life at Tralfamadore. This sub-alpine border land was like a gemstone found in a wonderful journey of discovery. We were entranced by the snow- capped mountain views and pristine streams. Wabisco, Bowen and Jingallalla join hands to become Deddick River, flowing into the Snowy river. My great delight was riding Katy up Warm Corners gully to follow fire trails. I found a special site to build my own tiny house.

Jingallalla

in the beginning
Jingallalla means 'singing stones'
the start of an incantation
pianissimo, yet guttural as
a one-year old's first burst of words
a valley vibrant with first words
and inklings of song

in this blissful stream
a myriad coloured pebbles
give us transparency

When the Camerons asked me to help rounding up cattle or sheep at the back of their property, I loved to ride bareback to be part of their team. The snow-clad peaks of Mt Kosciusko range were visible on the northern skyline. I recall riding home in an elevated state talking to emus or kangaroos, laughing and singing.

Gap

still the wind all but
lends me wings
as I ride warm tracks
bareback past a gap

three kangaroos
a panting dog
moving trees

sounds of branches cracking
a fence again
more parched bracken
sky moving south
collarbone streaks of snow
on Mt Tingaringi
clouds hovering
a log to jump
barbed wire to undo
strands of hair in my eyes
her stride picks up

familiar blue patch
something darker beyond
the last bend
slide off warm back
breathe in the scent
of her neck
home sweet home

14

Riding reveals a new world

*A*long the winding road to Tubbut, the Deddick river comes alive. When I am in a car, I trace the river with fleeting images, whereas on Katy, our rhythm follows the river. We float, we gush, whirl around a single stone, wind around sandbanks, tickle willow roots, glint at the sun and wink at passing cars - who hardly have a moment to see us.

Wildflowers surprise. Out of cracks in the granite, one purple trailing Hardenbergia vine, then no more for miles. One flower creamier than wattle, shaped like a star with a white tongue keeps pace with us. I am relieved that we are able to hear the occasional car from a distance, so that we can move into the gutter.

I sang in harmony with the river, and coming back, sang to soften the hard clay road.

This way of travel to Tubbut from Cabanandra gave me a sense of subtle changes in flora along the way as well as the pace and size of the river. We were attracted to the diversity of trees, from *Eucalptus macrohyncha* (stringybark) and *E. pauciflora* to *Callitris* pine and many different ti-tree, ferns and wattles. When Jurg and I started our native seed-collecting enterprise, Snowy River Seed, I became more attentive to the plants in different seasons. Birds joined the oratorio in different corners of the river as the annual rainfall reduced from 30 to 20 inches. At times I thought they were alerting birds downstream of our progress.

Tethered

tethered my mare
lit a fire, fed on the
brittle bits of ti-tree
hacked at today
on the site where my
house is to be, then
walked back facing yellow
sky till I met a fence
where my eye was wed
to snow-white heads
of the Cobbera range
distant yet sharper
than the barbs on the wire

Being in a place of our choice, with secret clear rivers and open space, views of stunning wilderness, with the freedom of moving from house to garden flat to tent on horseback, was a tonic after the heartbreak end to the first stay at Tralfamadore.

****

But all was not well in Camp Cabanandra.

My brother and I sat at the top of gully where we looked out at the Snowies quietly for a while. Then he said:

"Well I guess it's you or us. We can't all stay in the place together."

I said quickly: OK I will go. There's three of you with the baby Sam, and only one of me.

My heart sank, but I knew how hard it must have been for him.

Since 1972 we had lived together in the dilapidated old timber and fibro house, experienced the spring fire that terrified us and threatened the old house. I was out riding, gardening or fencing a lot of the time. Drought and unpredictable storms had been a constant. I worked with my brother on the fence around the flat garden.

Moonlight ride 1972

Those bony white trees
savour the moon's light
accent their curves
bend their knees

uphill it's rough twigs
on skin, sharp leaves
on cheek, deep holes
suddenly opening

river reflects moon
dilating behind white posts
that were trees once

after thrashing in dogwood
pony and I emerge
on the far side of our boundary
breathing ragged relief
too tired to look at the dimpled
flats, as we pick a blackberry
path beside broken posts
and dangling wire

moon, you nearly shone
through my bones
why was I scared to be alone
in your curtained arms?

I rode every day up the gully to look at the alpine views and sometimes did some stock work with the neighbours. Anyway, relationships became strained between the mother with a newborn baby and me.

15

The five-day long ride from Cabanandra to the NSW South coast

So in February 1973, late summer drought, I set off for Tralfamadore on the horse, with just a sack with a split in the middle slung across her back and a saddlebag, (recommended by the neighbouring farmer). I did not want to go through the trauma of her resistance to the float, and thought a long ride would be an adventure.

I was quietly hoping to meet up with my ex-lover Andre who was visiting there. All I carried in the sack was a change of clothes, some oats for Katy and some oats and rice for me. Tea and powdered milk maybe, a cup and plastic plate. A torch, a pocket- knife and matches...I must have had a sleeping bag too because I threw it on the ground to sleep in, more than once.

The horseback journey through East Gippsland, across the Monaro and down the Kybean Way to the Cobargo region was motivated by necessity, curiosity, and love. These three combined to give me energy, enthusiasm, and resilience.

From my diary: *Practical notes on how to start a journey through unknown territory in a drought for an unknown time towards a known destination for an unknown outcome.*

To pack in a split hessian sack as suggested by farmer next door:
the little radio (to pass time)
torch (to camp in the dark)
matches to light a forbidden flame
nuts to eat, oats for both horse and her girl
apples to catch the mare from anywhere
water for stretches between clean rivers
sleeping bag to hug the stars
running shoes for riding and crossings
notebook for noon musing and records of locals met
their answers to: how long since you seen the river this low?
do you like horses more than tractors?
were you born around here? Yes to all I am sure..
needle and cotton to patch broken spiderwebs
and forgotten dreams
envelopes and stamps to connect with scattered
bits of the world
tweezers for plucking thorns
long hair for keeping flies at bay
full moon for believing all will be revealed one day

today I realised I am strong
and can do who knows what
with whoever met
on foot, in jest, bareback
incognito, unlicensed
unbridled, unowned

in a whisper, out loud
alone, in a crowd
inside, outside, in hot or cold
however the whether strikes me....ride bold into the unknown Fiona

The first day was a hard slog, as we went along Bonang ridge where Katy kept turning her head to go back home. We stopped at the local store to stock up on a few Cherry-ripes, nuts and tea. Can I rely on local farmers to offer me milk? Then we left the so-called Bonang Highway unsealed road where the tree ferns drooped in the heat. 'Bendoc', said the sign.

We slogged up a long hill surrounded by waves of cricket sound. Then we descended into rainforest gullies where moisture still held on. I recall stopping for late lunch to let Katy graze on the sweet green grass near a creek. Wallabies and emus were our companions at times, not nervous about our presence. Please note that when I say 'we' it is Katy and I.

Only one four wheeled drive with Forestry workers passed us. Towards dusk we came to Bendoc outskirts. Small fibro timber workers' cottages stood looking haggard with porches sagging. Soon I noticed a grass tennis court behind a house, and decided to ask if I could let me pony stay in there the night rather than hobble her. The elderly woman was happy to let the horse mow the grass, and she came out to my tent in the morning to invite me for breakfast. She told me about her early days in Bendoc when she rode to Delegate for dances, and when they pulled logs with horses. This was the first but not the last generous hospitality I experienced on this journey.

As we clopped through Bendoc, past the school and the police station, a policeman emerged to talk to me. He asked where I had come from and where I was headed. He scratched his head, then went inside to bring me a canvas hat to make me look like a bushie, and he hoped, less like a young woman on her own. I thanked him for his thoughtful gesture, and assured him I would take care not to talk to strangers alone, or hitch a ride.

In reality, I had absolutely no fear of stranger danger. I chose to have faith in people. No amount of let-downs and betrayals would destroy this faith.

Next was a stop for morning tea at an old homestead. When I reached the Monaro Highway, a car pulled up with a couple in it. They asked how far it was to Bombala. I said "About half an hour by car, and would you mind taking this swag to the next bridge, so I can have a *canter*!"
They obliged with a chuckle, and off we cantered, putting Katy and I in a brighter mood.

Joy in the release of hooves in graceful alternating rhythm, sensing the muscles tense and relax, the minimal shifts in balance as she adjusts to rise and fall in the ground beneath. A miracle of movement that the rider can be in sync with so that the canter is flow, cushioned on air; weightless, wingless flight.

As promised, my swag saddlebags were beside the bridge. Luckily the saddlebags were hanging in clear view, and no one had stolen them. Out of the saddle-sacks came an apple to share with Katy.

A house set high above the river on my right beckoned to me. An elderly man opened the door. When he saw my horse tied up at the gate, he said:

Good afternoon. Harry Beveridge is my name. Where have you come from today?

Bendoc, I replied. My name is Fiona McIlroy. I am on my way to Cobargo.

He smiled, admired the pony, and took me inside for a cup of tea.

My daughter is taking care of me. My wife died last year. Old age. She was 92. Sad.

When I asked politely if he could tell me his age, he said 95. Not old at all… he smiled.

After his daughter (73 perhaps) brought the tea, we sat talking. He told me he used to work on the roads with horse drawn equipment, and loved working with horses. He also recalled riding home from a night at Bendoc pub, splayed on the back of the horse, safely arriving home.

Then he started to reminisce about the gold rush in Bendoc and Craigie. He talked about spending time with the Chinese who grew vegetables, dug channels for the water from the Bonang river to sluice for gold, and he recalled playing cards with them in their tents.

His daughter, who seemed to slur her words, clearly under the influence, insisted on telling me how the Chinese were 'quaite naice' people, and how her daughter was in business with them in Hong Kong.

From the gold rush in Craigie and Bendoc, we went on into the unknown, feeling a bit of time warp.

At Bombala, I stopped at the bakery, then found the farrier Mr Black. By this time, poor Katy had worn her hooves down, and was a bit tender on the bitumen or gravel. He shod her, almost bringing her to her knees when she pulled away. He had hit a tender spot on the frog. I was shocked by his ruthlessness. However, the bottom line was she had to be shod before we went on.

After that trauma was over, Katy had a spring in her step. We were heading for Nimmitabel, across the notoriously monotonous Monaro Plateau. I was fascinated by every undulation, every clump of grass. Each living thing seemed to be part of a natural symphony with light, wind and time accompanied by occasional sound.

Now we felt the prolonged drought. The grass was thin across the balding scalp of the land, stretched taut as far as the eye can see. Monaro highway snaked up and down the undulating plateau, while Katy delicately picked her way along the thin strip of gravel between the bitumen and the sward. Cars were irregular, but when they came, it was at least 100 km an hour, and drivers did not often slow down; in fact the drivers sometimes looked back as if they had only recognized an equine road apparition after leaving us in their shuddering wake. Fortunately Katy did not flinch as the utes and 4wds swooped past so close her hair ruffled. It was mid-afternoon when we reached the wide river at Bibbenluke. I had a dip to cool off, and a rest under the bridge, while Katy enjoyed the rare green pick along the riverbank.

At five, as the sun eased its intense glare, we set off again towards the Ando after a stiff but gradual climb. I recall the pleasure of seeing every small change in the cloud, and the shadow on the barren hills. As well, I began to realise that animals noticed us, even from hundreds of metres distance, lifting their heads to sniff, and bellowing or baaing. But the horses were interested enough to sniff the wind, then set off at a good pace across the paddock, to pull up at the fence near where Katy waited with baited breath. Later, I realized the low whickering and quivering were signs of being in season, and ready for love!

At Ando, we turned in to a farmhouse with a large water tank. I knocked at the door, and the farmer came out. He offered Katy a bucket of water, and to my eternal chagrin, she tipped it over. Not good enough for this mare, even in a drought! She had only drunk a bit at the Bibbenluke river near Bombala in the morning, so I was worried. I apologized to the farmer on her behalf, and we went over the road to enter a droving reserve for the evening. I had intended to sleep in the drover's hut, but we were so tired, I unsaddled her and dropped my sleeping bag on the tussock. I did not even hobble her, but in the starry night I noticed she grazed around me in ever-increasing circles as if I were her anchor. No more need for hobbles!

The bond between the horse and I kept deepening. The most amazing part was to come. As she came in season, her body language changed. Her ears constantly pricked and moving, her head held high, occasional nickering to greet a horse that came up to the fence. I felt how alert she was, and how alive. Wondering if she was in season but surprised, because the last time I took her to a stallion nothing happened, and the farmer shook his head, saying she is too old at fourteen. However....being an optimist and responding to her obvious interest in the boys....geldings came up in zigzag, while colts came up like a bolt out of the blue.

16

Nearly down the cliff

Nearing Nimmitabel, we had a near-death experience. It began to rain, drought-breaking welcome rain. I wanted to avoid the splash of cars roaring past, so we went to the left of the white railing over a gully. Suddenly, the ground gave way and she lost her hind legs, suspended over the gully below for a few seconds before she lunged forward to leap over the white railing, knocking my leg as she did. Aching and swearing at the swooping cars, I managed to keep moving.

Then just before Nimmitabel we spotted a colt who was very amorous. I looked around, saw no farmhouse, and opened a gate, let the mare in to greet him. What a romantic interlude followed; nothing like what takes place at a paid gig, where the mare is backed into a chute, and the stallion has his way while she squeals protest. This was different. Idyllic. They nibbled each other's mane, whispered sweet nothings into nostrils, reared up and clasped each other with forelegs. Lots of foreplay. Although, it was a challenge to catch her. Afterwards, we arrived at Nimmitabel very wet and tired. Stopped at the baker, who owned the Nimmitabel Inn across the road. He said he had a room for a horse and her girl. He then offered to tether her in the only patch of green clover in the town next to the bakery. He was very keen to hear some stories from the ride, and brought me some bread and hot tea in a lovely room near the top with dormer windows and a small fireplace. I slept like a log.

Next day I was happy to see children stroking Katy's neck, and talking to her. I placed a few on her back. The baker wanted to hear my stories over breakfast, and told me about the landholders on the Kybean Way on my way to the escarpment where the fire trail descends to Cobargo via Yowrie.

We set off feeling much refreshed and appreciative of the Nimmitabel Baker and the hospitality. My bruised leg was quick to heal. On the way to the escarpment, we noticed a lively young thoroughbred bay colt at the fence. Katy melted, nickering and quivering. She clearly had more to share!

I decided to go in to the farmhouse. An older farmer came to the door. I said: my mare likes your colt. Do you mind if I let her in to meet him?

He said: he is about to get the chop, so let's give them a chance. Come in and have lunch with us, we can keep an eye on them.

So I let her in. Katy and the colt reared up in an embrace, then cantered about, whinnying and enjoying foreplay. Meanwhile, I enjoyed roast Sunday lunch with two very friendly people. He came with me to help catch Katy. She was loath to leave her new Romeo.

We quickstepped our way to the Nimmitabel station that the baker had recommended we stop to say hallo. We were invited to stay the night when they heard my story. I swam in the river, and met the 11 year old girl who claimed to be the aunt of the newborn baby. Had trouble working that out. Hospitality was high-class however.

17

Steep descent to Wadbilliga

*N*ext morning we set off early as the fire trail was said to be a risky ride. We reached the headwaters of the Wadbilliga river, then descended via a steep, rocky fire trail. I can recall the amazing views of the forested slopes, and how I had to dismount in order to prevent the saddle slipping down her neck, as we did not have a crupper between the saddle and her tail. An unforgettable experience on the edge of the earth.

On reaching the lower ground, we visited a farm near Yowrie, where I knew the farmers from my previous stay at Tralfamadore. From there, we made it to Yowrie PO, and then started the long hilly track over six river crossings of the Wadbilliga to reach Tralfamadore. By this time, Katy and I were best friends. Her hoofbeat, the flicking of her ears were in rhythm with my humming.

By that time, I knew that heart-breaker Andre had left Tralfamadore to return to Sydney with no attempt to contact me. He actually waved at Nimmitabel as he drove past Katy and I- just as we turned out of town toward the escarpment. This made me realise he had shut the door on any renewal of our relationship. I had to become an independent woman able to sustain myself without a man. Even without understanding what had happened to the most intimate love affair where I had trusted that the love between us broke all records, and went beyond sexual preferences. I still held a flame for him for years. Still I refused to close the door on love.

In some ways, this ride on the horse was not only an adventure with more risk than many would undertake, requiring trust in the world and myself as well as the horse. However, part of my motivation was to meet up with my ex-lover near the place we had been together. When he left Tralfamadore without so much as a message, my trust in the world, in him, in love was shattered again.

To continue the quest for whatever the journey brought, took a different kind of courage. I recall at Nimmitabel when he went past with just a wave, I felt my whole being rattled as if a cold wind blew through me. Then I made a choice. To continue living as if I was worthwhile, and to be wholehearted about continuing my journey. The horse was so alive, in her zenith, that I focused on her life force. I almost fused with her sense of zeal and energy. The mare and I were in love with life. Attuned to each other's moods and cycles. So much so that for many years afterward, I knew the exact day of her cycle to conceive a foal.

Settling in to the lovely Brassknocker Creek, Katy and I enjoyed taking Tralf children around from river flat to river flat when parents left them in my care, and taking the horse in the river.

18

The lesson about shielding myself from objects of fear

*T*he beautiful black and white foal was born at Tralfamadore, despite many refusing to believe that a one-hour lunch stop with a colt could result in a foal. I even convinced myself that her barrel had swollen from gorging on luscious green grass. Poor Katy! Therefore when the filly appeared, she was a great gift.

After a few weeks the filly grew in boldness and agility. Sometimes she turned her back and kicked out in play, or ran to nip as if I was another foal, a playmate. I began to be nervous, and wondered if this would encourage her to keep nipping and kicking. So I pondered a solution to this. Susan Jeffers' advice is to 'Feel-the-Fear and do it anyway'. However this approach does not address the present and increasing danger of real injury. Katy had her ways of disciplining Lunar, but no voice of mine would deter her.

The next idea was to place a barrier between Lunar and me. I proceeded to construct a yard out of fallen branches. Then every day I brought Katy and her foal into the yard, and managed to brush, stroke and handle Lunar while the fence protected me. For the risk-averse, it is wise not to try if you're scared. I felt that my discovery on that day would be helpful in many situations, where I might want to flee perceived danger, but achieve something by taking steps to minimize risk. Surely even Pollyanna would try to get help to put out the fire before jumping in to rescue someone!

19

Trusting the horse - surrender to total darkness

Before Lunar was born, I took on the duty of going out to Yowrie PO to collect the mail once a week. It was an enjoyable challenge to ride six kilometres over six river crossings in all weather. As well, I didn't like the thought of driving a 4 wheel drive on slippery or rocky roads, making the track more treacherous and sometimes leading to a puncture, running out of fuel, scaring the wildlife. I could commune with the birds, and pass wallabies or dragon lizards without causing them alarm. Or squashing them….

One particular day, I arrived at the usual early afternoon time. The mail had been delayed. I chatted to the owner of the post office about local politics and potatoes. At last, the mailman arrived, and Katy and I set off about 4.30 for Tralfamadore. As we crossed the first crossing, cloud came over the moon. It was suddenly dark. I was frightened, trying to discern shapes of rocks to signal the path edge. Then I realized Katy could see much better than me. She did not seem to hesitate, but without stumbling, pick her way along the path gently. I decided the choices were limited. I could not sleep on the hard ground. I could not see where we were going. So I chose to close my eyes and surrender to her powers of navigation in the dark. It was a transformative experience. Perhaps being a meditation guru brings this depth of surrender.

Years of meditation practice could have led me to this. But being an impatient seeker of peak experiences (to use my sister's lingo), I found a way to get there by dint of a combination of chance and choice….I would recommend this to everybody, but the occasion cannot really be easily repeated. Synchronicity perhaps.

Katy brought me to my little home on the Brassknocker Creek without misadventure. I felt like I was in a physical body joined to hers, with the rhythm of her gait enmeshed in my heart's rhythm. I probably hummed to the rhythm. I was aware of the danger of dropping off to sleep in the saddle. So I kept myself in a hypnotic state but still sang or murmured to stay awake and to keep in touch with the horse. I still recall crossing the river with the sounds and sensations amplified by the lack of visual stimuli. This required the most attention, without panic, as the horse had to focus totally on keeping her footing. Hats off to Katy!

20

Nethercote

After living in an army tent, gardening and helping to care for children in the community, I decided to move to a lovely place living with my cousin Angela and friends in a house closer to facilities, including access to employment. Having ridden from Tralfamadore to Nethercote near Pambula with the 8 month old foal beside me via fire trails and back roads, without an overnight stop, I was relieved to arrive at my cousin's farm nestled into the green slopes. They had invited me to stay for as long as I liked.

Their life seemed easier than ours at Tralfamadore or Cabanandra, as they were more connected to town facilities, eg library, shops, markets, other neighbours, school. I even taught sometimes at the local primary school and at the local library. This helped me to get my Diploma of Education a year later.

We grew vegetables in the rich volcanic soil, enjoying selecting the vegetables we loved to plant and care for. Angela's two sons were there at the time. Angela John and I enjoyed a close trio relationship with mutual massage and lying listening to music together before bed; an idyllic alternative lifestyle.

Meanwhile, I bought another horse at the Cobargo market. He was going to be sold to the knackers, so I was told. I had connected with him by breathing into his nostril, and he calmed down. Then we found out he was half-draught, half-thoroughbred. He had been a show-jumper but had gone off it. I tried riding him bareback and discovered he was comfortable as a rocking horse. Soon after I brought him to Nethercote, we tried him in the shafts with a single furrow plough and a harrows. He had to be led, and one day he began to trot and got away from John, straight through a fence until the gear tangled up and broke his harness. That was the end of his potential career with us. I took him back and sold him at the market as a riding horse. At least an advance from a destiny at the knackers!

Katy and I continued to enjoy rides along fire trails. The filly Lunar came along. I still recall a beautiful experience when the filly was stretched out on the ground asleep. I decided to trim her hooves then, and she allowed me to pick up each hoof and file it, until I got to the last hoof when she woke suddenly and sprang up. Risky podiatry idea....

21

Lost and found

One day I felt Katy was telling me she was ready for the stallion. The filly was at least a year old by then, so we could leave her at the farm. I set off with a map showing the fire trails to Brogo. It was a long trek along a rough pebbly trail. Mainly along a ridge towards the left shoulder of Mountain. After an hour or two, we seemed to be heading to the right of the Mountain. I was a bit puzzled, since I had followed the map and the sign for the fire trail. As well, I had heard stories about people disappearing into caves at the top of the Mountain, and it seemed that we were being drawn towards the summit. To cap it off, Katy had begun to show signs of being footsore, walking carefully, and stumbling occasionally.

A wave of determination made me decide to turn off the track down the rocky hillside, to avoid the mysterious pull of the sacred mountain. Katy was amazingly amenable, and clambered down towards the gully with strong willpower. I can recall pulling a fallen barbed wire fence apart, which shows how desperate I was. (My diary says I tied it together again!) We found ourselves on the road very close to the junction with the road to Burragate and Wandello.

Another miracle happened, when my friend drove up at the agreed time at the junction. I had thought we were hours late.

That evening we arrived at the farm where the stallion lived. Katy had been feeding her filly now being weaned at 18 months. I lit a tiny campfire for tea, and put a cup under her bulging breasts to try some mare's milk. The best cuppa in history!

She was happy to have an encounter with the stallion. It must have been the right timing as we did not stay to see whether she needed a second go. Even though I was still mystified how we got lost under Mt Darragh, I was curious to go back trying to follow the route as per the map.

More mystery, but this time less scary. Our route took us to the right shoulder of Mt Darragh and then down to cross a lovely creek, before a straightforward path along a ridge through Wadbilliga National Park, and home to Tralfamadore. I had to take my hat off to the indigenous ancestors for releasing us without any further drama. Even so, I never understood how we took completely different routes there and return. I wonder if anyone else can tell me how we went astray…and didn't disappear!

☙ 22 ❧

A break in the journey.

Realising I needed to be able to teach at the local schools of Tubbut, Goongerah and Bendoc, I decided to do a year at UNE to complete a Dip Ed.in 1975. I reluctantly left Katy and her miracle foal Lunar behind. Then in February after reaching Armidale, a call came through from Nethercote telling me that Lunar had had a bad accident. The vet said she would be lame all her life. This gave me a reason to give up the Dip Ed, but as fate would have it, I fell ill with flu and could not drive. The twists of fate continued till in 3rd term, after writing a letter of despair about the horror of prac teaching Year 8-9 classes in Murwillumbah, I had a serious spinal fracture. A veranda railing collapsed at a teacher's house near Murwillumbah. Lying on the ground I recall staring at the stars thinking 'is this the only way to end this horror?' This accident led to two weeks in hospital, and somehow managing to complete the Diploma from bed.

I returned to my beloved home at Cabanandra. Unfortunately, nerve pain between crushed vertebra was a constant companion from then on. Sitting more than an hour, lifting and carrying triggered it. Sadly this meant I had to set limits to riding time, and gardening. This continued till children entered the picture.

23

Tim: the rescued Clydesdale

We always wanted to farm without petrol driven modern machinery. I longed to work the soil with a horse driven plough and harrows. Brother Bob and I heard there were draught horses being used to pull pine logs on the Monaro.

I was hitch hiking when I heard about a young horse that bolted with a log in tow and they put him in a paddock. I went out to look for Tim (short for Timber). Bob went to pick him up and found one horse had died and another had run away into the Pine forest. I decided to go with Dr Bob and we brought back an injured young Clydesdale Tim to his place. There he treated his damaged mouth and badly swollen fetlocks from chains.

I was furious with the company employees for their abuse of the horses. When Tim's wounds healed we trucked Tim to Cabanandra. We groomed him and fed him till he no longer flinched at our touch. Over time we introduced the bridle with blinkers, and then the harness. He was very nervous about that. Anything flapping or pinching made him jump. I decided to try riding him bareback to restore his trust in us. That was a good idea, and he became a safe and relaxed steed. Mounting him required a good stump or a good leg-up, but once on always bareback, Tim was a dream.

Sadly Tim never really recovered from his trauma from cruel handling. We could never be sure when a sudden flap or pressure from harness would snap him into hyper-alert state, when he would take off with no regard for the veggie plot. Eventually we decided to sell him to a local who was training a team for the Bendoc show. As we had hoped, being in a team calmed him and he managed to restore himself.

However, we never had a Clydesdale and had to make do with Katy, and later her successor Cypress.

To quote from an article I wrote:

You can teach an old pony new tricks (Pub.Local Rag Tubbut)

Katy had never been in shafts before I tied two poles to the stirrups, and she pulled them down a hill without bailing. Later, when we had two acres of buckwheat on the Pest Flat, we tied two eucalypt branches to her stirrups, and she happily harrowed the rows of buckwheat after my friend mounted her. After the crop was harvested, I slung sheaves across her back and rode bareback up the hill to the shearing shed

After a year of searching, I had bought a lovely red sulky while returning from the coast. It cost $150, which at the time nearly broke the bank. This sulky was a very treasured vehicle. I trained Katy with patience and staying near her head. She never bolted with it! She was ready to roll within a day or two of being led. Children loved being on board, but we had to learn from a couple of near-disasters that it is not all plain sailing.

The furthest I ever went with the sulky was Tubbut, and the main obstacle was the occasional car or truck roaring round a blind bend, with a near collision on the agenda. But the regular trip was over to Warm Corners or to Bob and Deb's or up to Cecily's house on the ridge. I absolutely loved the sulky, and so did the kids. Sadly, one day a young friend who was staying with us, turned her too sharply near a fence, and the sulky overturned. Luckily my daughter and the girl were thrown free of the vehicle and the frightened mare. Katy would not pull a sulky again. Her mouth was torn, and she fled.

Later the lovely buckskin Cypress would take the sulky to meet the preschool teacher with Bonny age 4, at the corner of the Tubbut and Dellicknora Roads. The teacher then drove Bonny into Delegate.

Patched sky

moon full of cheek
wind rakes hill
we shelter in the armpit
of Warm Corners Gully
the skewbald and I
waiting for the tree symphony
to reach its climax

moving on we find
a white-limbed tree
in its prime, broken
half-way down its spine
naked under my boots
distance speaks louder
than crunch of heartbreak

watching the path of the wind
through its chosen leaves
on the far ridge
my eyes catch
in the patched sky

✶ 24 ✶

Back to Cabanandra 1974

I had decided to return to Cabanandra, my spiritual home. Our mother bought the block of 354 acres on the other side of the Jingallalla from the original land we had bought.

Somehow being back there in the mountains after living in the coastal valley of Nethercote felt right, even though the climate was more challenging. Once I began a canter from the Co-op Wabisco creek across the paddocks, and as I came up to the gate, it was like a dream- where the gate represented the entry or exit to waking state. Amazing experience, expressed in a poem. (Warm Corners, 2002 Ginninderra Press)

The joy of canter- the gate

eyes rest soft on pillow
of horizon

slow and regular hoofbeat
on the brow of the hill

suddenly- a gate

heartbeat rises
to meet the now-
brought up short before
tomorrow

Excerpt 1980 (published Earth Garden 1980)

I first spotted Katy round as a barrel in a paddock near Kinglake, eating her head off. 'She needs riding, will you come once a week? 'asked the family who looked after her while their daughter was at uni in Melbourne. 'Too much of a good life can ruin a pony. She has already foundered, due to the juicy grass and disuse.' Katy was happy to be caught. It seemed a shame to me that a fit healthy pony could become disabled because the owner who loved her, could no longer ride her. In her later years, Katy became lame again, and this was a sad end to her otherwise fit and full life.

Fortunately for Katy, her owner was weeping tears of relief when I offered to buy her. I handed her the 120 pounds and she handed me the bridle, across a Laminex table in a city café. She said: 'Katy is a willing and kind pony. Just keep her exercised and use her mouth gently. She will never bite or kick.'

As I walked away down the street, I happened to notice a sign above a shop doorway saying: Save petrol, buy a horse'....that struck me as a good omen. Certainly, I did not buy a car while I lived in the bush with Katy. Admittedly I had a few lifts and hitchhiked. However, it is possible to gear down your expectations of speed and time sufficiently to manage life on horseback even when it is rare. But it does demand imagination, a few bales of hay, and consistent awareness that your transport vehicle is alive! Over the 15 years with Katy, I discovered she was capable of learning a host of new tricks.

Each horse or pony has a unique personality. Katy was the quietest horse I had ever met. She never even laid her ears back at a human, let alone bit or kicked. However, she knew her mind. When it came time to load Katy into a horse float to bring her up to our farm in far East Gippsland from Melbourne, she managed to resist passively for six hours. With inducement of oats, with blindfold, lifting her legs one by one, with voice and pressure of ropes, she refused to budge past the ramp.

At last, I had to call a vet to give her an anaesthetic. (I had tried to avoid taking her such a long distance while she was out of it..) Even then, it took all the aforementioned aids, to bring her one leg at a time, into the dreaded float. Thank goodness she never had to travel in a float again. In fact, that was one reason why I set off from far East Gippsland in the foothills of the Snowies to near Cobargo on the South coast of NSW. We had to go, even though it was a severe drought summer. Katy was fat, but any worries about the feasibility of such a long ride evaporated after the second day. Riding through rainforest from Bonang was deeply nourishing. The first night in Bendoc, Katy had a luxury stay in an overgrown tennis court. In the morning I was invited to breakfast, and heard many stories about the history of Bendoc, with tales of horses and riders that would make Katy pale. On the second day, Katy had her ears pricked forward and was alert to the road ahead. We met an endless stream of herbivores from sheep to horses, curious enough to come up to the fence.

I found myself singing, and observing the paths of birds and clouds with growing interest. We stopped for a cuppa in shady places, and Katy munched happily wherever there was green grass.

My only concern was the design of the modern highway meant we could not safely ride on the verges, but had to ride on the gravel next to the road. Drivers never slackened speed, but swept down the hill to pass us so close that they nearly shaved the hair on our legs. The cuttings with their white railings and rubble filled gullies were not designed with horse travel in mind. I wondered how farmers fared who wanted to ride between large paddocks to move stock. What, I asked myself, was the point of buying a horse to save petrol, if you couldn't stay alive on the roads.

From that five day ride, Katy gained a filly foal from a half hour stand in a paddock with a thoroughbred colt. I noticed she was very keen to meet up with him, and stood shaking in anticipation. I knocked on the farmhouse door, and the farmer kindly asked me in for a lamb roast cooked by his wife. We watched the courtship from the window, and luckily caught the mare after her fling. I gained a sense of trusting my companion on the road, and a sense of liberation in travelling on my own. Katy would graze in small circles around me, close to my tent, and was always willing to be caught. It is an entirely different experience from driving a car between Oodnadatta and Alice Springs, where you are cocooned from the outside world. On horseback I learned to experience every inch of the vast Australian landscape. The stars were a vital part of the picture every night.

25

Moving forward yet falling backwards

As it turned out, I would bend over backwards, literally and metaphorically, with a broken spine.

Conceding that I needed a meal ticket to continue my horse-based country life, I went to gain a Diploma of Education at UNE, at my ancestral home Armidale. Soon after arriving to stay with relatives, a message from Cabanandra told me that Lunar, Katy's foal (the precious foal born from the long ride) had broken her leg in a fence. At that moment, it seemed imperative to go back and take care of her. However, I got a bad flu and could not travel for three weeks. By that time, the urgency of her care had eased. So I stayed in Armidale.

On return to the lovely farm in far East Gippsland, my horse riding was much limited. I could ride short distances, but no more long rides. However, this pony had multifarious purposes. For example, one time I had attached some poles for the frame of a small home, to her stirrups, and she dragged them down a slope to the site. She gave birth to two foals. Six years later, Katy died. She is still very much alive to me.

Next, we placed her in a lovely red sulky that I had managed to track down, and I stayed at her head until she grew accustomed to it. She never shied or kicked at it. Nor did she worry about the endless fumblings with the harness and the long reins. Even with her amenable nature, I would recommend finding an experienced person to induct you before introducing a green horse into harness. In our early days, with overblown confidence, we set off with Katy and sulky up a gravelly hill, her first hill.

She stopped, jibbed, then backed dangerously close to the edge of the cutting. One friend valiantly pushed the sulky, while I coaxed and clicked at her head. The straps were so taut I couldn't undo them at first, and it looked like pony and sulky overboard. If you take a step before you and the horse are fully ready, you may regret it. Even Katy, the quietest pony in the known universe, landed us in a perilous situation. The sulky, however, was an absolute favourite with the children, my own and others. It was reasonably safe to travel on country roads since you could hear a car coming and move to the side. Mind the gutter though.

Still, that doesn't compare with the cost of keeping a car running. A horse is cheap by comparison, except when agistment is needed. Ride around checking your boundary fences, do stockwork with your neighbours, take a child behind or in front, canter bareback for the joy of the motion.

I feel it is best for both pony and child to lead them or ride double until they have enough balance to avoid seesawing on the horse's mouth. It is natural when learning to ride with reins in hand, to pull the reins as a means of keeping balance. Some ponies at riding schools have mouths like iron, from too much of this. Once the child is comfortable to sit at the trot, it is possible to give the reins to the new rider.

A mare can have foal after foal, especially if she is a good doer, like Katy, needing to feed more than one. I kept riding her gently until weeks before foaling, and then again soon after the foal is born. It is possible to handle the foal until rapport is established, although care needs to be taken if it treats you like a playmate, and turns to kick you! There are infinite ways to develop mutual trust and respect between a pony and you. Please, don't join the ranks of owners who leave their beloved ponies unridden to founder in their paddocks. On the other hand, don't leave your pony to starve in a tiny paddock in a drought. A pony eats twice as much as a cow. Think of the pony as a friend, a good way of travelling, a strong assistant, and a link with nature. If we are serious about conserving our scarce resources, and minimizing pollution, we can not only buy a horse, but respect its value for your lifestyle. Riding is not recreation. As I see it, riding a horse is travelling in style.

26

The eclipse

Returning from a particularly challenging week teaching at the Orbost High School, I was looking forward to a family celebration barbecue and viewing of the solar eclipse. Driving down my mother's drive, I spotted Katy at the fence gazing with head up towards Bonang. I leapt out of the car and greeted her. With a shudder of recognition, I decided it was time to go to meet the stallion at Bonang. What an adventure- riding through the forest along the old ridge road while a full eclipse takes place! Ignoring my sense of obligation to be with others, I took a water bottle and the bridle, and set off. She was stepping out brightly. It was about five pm when we set off. Sunset would normally take place about seven.

A little way along the Old Bonang road, I looked up as the light was different, and saw the sun with a chip out of it, and as the bite kept steadily eating into the sun, I saw kookaburras, magpies, and small finches darting around madly, and the birdsong sped up so that the kookaburras evening chortle became a mad goon version. I chortled along with them, and observed all the wildlife hastening pace to keep up with what they may have thought was an early bedtime. By the time I reached some yards near Bonang, the hullabaloo from lowing cattle was deafening. By this time, there was only a fingernail of the sun left. The farmers were shouting as the cattle stamped and bellowed in panic.

What an experience. Unforgettable and unimaginable. We do not often wonder how the rest of the animal world reacts to unusual events in the galaxy!

Then, on reaching the farm where the stallion waited, the union was immediate. Katy was ready to conceive. No need to wait around three weeks as is the usual routine. But this time I left her there just to prove to myself and others that we had known the moment.

27

Katy pulling logs

When Jurg and I had ceased being a couple, I resolved to build a little place of my own. With the help of two ex-partners,(believe it or not) we made a makeshift harness with ropes through stirrups, and with a bowsaw cut some stringybark logs. Then we attached the logs to the ropes and walked Katy down the hill to the site. There we dug holes, put in stumps and used the poles as joists. This was as far as we got with my single status dwelling. Heritage structure to this day…eternally incomplete.

After we had agreed to stop trying to be a couple, Jurg and I went together to Melbourne and lived with a good friend who was working in a library at the time. I worked on an Aboriginal literacy program in Dandenong where we used Kevin Gilbert's 'Living Black' book as a text.

One of my students went to Latrobe Uni to work. Next week she rang me to say: guess what? Kevin Gilbert is looking for another research assistant and he wants to meet you.

I was interviewing women in communities, like Yirrkala and Yuendumu where often women produced art, danced and sang. I learnt about the health issues, the education and work challenges, domestic violence and alcohol of course. The women were leaders in the community. This project was a very valuable one.

~ 28 ~

The bountiful harvest - Katy harrowing and carrying sheaves of buckwheat straw 1973

*W*e at Cabanandra were keen to grow as much of our own food as possible, and we knew the original owners in early 1900s grew barley, but we decided to try buckwheat as it was a shorter crop and we chose it for its health properties. We had a flat that was fondly referred to as the pest flat mainly for its prolific blackberries and rabbits. We wanted to try horse-power, so without proper horse drawn equipment we had to improvise. We tied two long branches to the stirrups. Jurg hopped on Katy and rode her along the furrows. I then took a turn. She was very cooperative, and after the seed was thrown out very peasant style by Jurg and I, she harrowed the rows successfully. We were very happy when the seedlings popped up.

A few months later, the crop was laden with buckwheat seed, so out came the scythe in the best Swiss hands. My mother Cecily had a clever idea to thresh the grain. We rolled an old water tank into the corner and the harvested sheaves were bashed against the sides of the tank so that the grain fell to the floor. My favourite mission was to load Katy with sheaves of buckwheat stalks in donkey style, and ride her up the steep hill to the shearing shed.

The buckwheat made wonderful pancakes and porridge for us, and great hay for the cows and horses. Ah those were the days my friend we thought they'd never end...

I think we only harvested twice on the Pest flat (later re-named Best flat) before things started to unravel with the fabric of our personal and social lives, partly due to the growing pressure about the owner-built house from the building surveyor.

29

Weeta the wallaby

One day in summer holidays, I found a wallaby on the side of the road and got off the horse to check the pouch. I found a very young joey, almost without fur. Wrapping it in a scarf, I took it home safely not very certain how long it would live. Fortunately . a neighbour had the marsupial milk needed, in powder form and a tiny bottle. Then began the amazing journey of Weeta (named after my mother's auntie)and me. When the black wallaby had fur, but before she could hop around, I set off to visit Tralfamadore for a special event. I did not want to drive, but took a lift, and then hitched from Delegate. When I got in the car with my leather shoulder bag and rucksack, I did not know whether to let the driver know we had an added hitchhiker at first, but when Weeta stuck her neck out, I introduced her. They were enchanted....they dropped me at Cann Valley Hotel at dusk. Again I did not announce her presence when I booked a single room. She was so modest and low impact that I thought she would not present a problem, but thought that their policy would not permit pets in the room.

All went swimmingly that night, even slept while I went to the bar for a wine and burger...in the morning I ducked down the hall for a quick shower, but when I came back the cleaner had entered my room and was chortling and exclaiming about the little wallaby exploring the room. She asked if the hotelier knew and when I said "no please don't tell", she humoured me and said: "I promise"...and bless her she didn't tell the hotelier. I did though. Once he saw her little pixie face he was a goner, and I was forgiven.

Thus began my charmed life cohabiting with Weeta at Tralfamadore on Brassknocker Creek in a large army tent. By day she mosied around the tent and sniffed about the river bank. In the evening when I lit the fire outside for cooking an evening meal, Weeta would leap up into her black pouch and I would carry her around till bedtime. So I slept in the sleeping bag with her little warm body curled up near my tummy. I recall wondering if this was the closest I would come to being a mum.

There were several young settlers along the Brassknocker valley Whom I visited and did some activities with. One cluster had two dogs. I asked if they tied up the dogs at night, or kept them inside. I was told with a grin: No....why would we? If dogs run free why cant we? I explained that I heard dogs howling especially around full moon as they hunted at night.

I told them that my wallaby was likely to be an easy target.

Not my dogs … was the glib reply.

Next evening I returned from a gathering just after dark, and could not find Weeta. I called and searched as the moon rose. She had disappeared. I was angry with what I felt was a blatant pet-centric rose-tinted glasses attitude. Allowing dogs to 'run free' at the expense of a small precious native marsupial life.

30

Not listening to my heart-broken bones 1975

*M*y first instinct was to go back and give up on the teaching qualification. My father's voice told me again to be strong, to persist on the career path. I felt this injury was a signal to stay on my path with the horse for a guide...at first. However, my cold worsened, and left the window to go back closed...now all I could do was remember the Serenity Prayer...strength to change the things I can, let go of the things I can't, and the wisdom to know the difference.....

What would I have done in hindsight? I explore this in my chapter in Path to Wellness (Pub titled: *A break in the journey* is about recovery from trauma by conscious choice or by harsh reminder.

After sending off the chapter to the publisher , I had an experience that sorely tested my resilience and almost made me believe the 'you create your life doctrine'.

My message in the chapter was to pause when you are pushing yourself beyond reason to achieve a goal. Then reflect on whether the goal is true to your core values. A common saying is 'this will make or break you.'

My experience has been that pursuing a goal that was causing mental distress can be followed by a serious accident that on reflection, is almost a relief compared to continuing the path we were on. This happened when I was doing prac teaching and wrote a letter to my best friend saying this is the most crushing tormenting experience of my life...that evening at a teachers party, a verandah railing collapsed and I fell six feet, causing a crush fracture of my spine. I persisted and finished my Dip Ed on my back in bed on pain killers.

A year later, travelled two hours each way to teach at Orbost High school, fearing and feeling unable to manage the raw classroom behaviour, I had three car accidents before I finally decided high school was not my bag. So pushing myself to pursue a goal that was unsuited to my nature led to nasty outcomes. Was there a link? It seemed a bit too fatalistic or deterministic even for a faint mystic like me. But if it was just the inadvertent use of language such as a 'break' in the journey, that would be a cruel calculating vengeful God.

So when I drove down from Canberra in 2014, to our beautiful Jingallalla after fierce fires burnt down dwellings, followed by floods that swept away bridges, I was feeling devastated. Walking up and down hills near the river, the ground gave way under my left leg, and snapped the tibia. Only by luck I managed to alert a neighbour, and eventually taken four hours to Emergency in Canberra, resulting in a rod in the leg.

While in hospital I twigged that I had titled my chapter A break in the journey!! Was it possible to cause an accident just by using a word? After a near mental breakdown, I decided no. Accidents are not always caused by our own negligence or attitude. There are other factors at play in our lives, such as climate change or a pure collision of time and space. Or a moment of distraction.

31

Timing- Katy's last breath on the pine needles

In the last year of teaching at Goongerah and Tubbut, I recall that Katy was always grazing happily on the hillside when I returned. She was a 'good doer', and never got thin or ribby even in the harshest winter. Except for the year when she was 29 years old. This was 1989- a harsh winter and early spring. The grass was green and rich, but I was surprised to see Katy up close to the yards as if she wanted to tell me something.

That night was a full moon, and I woke. For some unknown reason, I got up, got dressed and walked across the Jingallalla and up to the stand of old cypress. There was Katy lying on her side. Her head did not move. I sat down near her. Her eyes were still open. I felt she was cool to the touch. Bending down, I placed my nose in front of her nostrils, and shared a breath like a sigh. This was to be her final breath. I lay against her body and cried. Amazed that she had waited till I arrived, to take her last breath. An absolutely intimate and unique shared transition from life to death. If ever I doubted that love exists, this kiss dispensed with that doubt.

Later, with the father of my son, we had some adventures with the lovely Cypress, who had inordinate patience and tolerance with children. Double-dinking was very popular with me in front and child behind.

32

Honeysuckle Range – a family trek by horse and donkey –

I was anxious to the point of snapping when we were ready to leave. "No saddles?! No neckstraps for the girls to hold on? No backpack in case Bo gets sick of horse riding? This is a crazy expedition. And you just say 'it'll be alright, let's go'? I recalled the last time an adult had told me everything would be alright – and my horse had died.

Jumping onto the pony bareback, with a blanket over her back, is no mean feat. It resulted in a bunched-up blanket under me, or a blanket behind me, or falling over the other side. Bowen's dad gave me a leg up, so strong that it nearly landed me over the other side of the mare. She insisted on moving off before we were ready.

Travelling with two donkeys and a horse presents a few challenges. The donkeys will follow behind the horse, but if the horse is behind them, the donkeys scurry off at a fast jog in panic. Thus, when going through gates, strict etiquette must be observed.

The pony must stand well away from the gate and wait, while someone opens the gate and brings the donkeys through. Then Cypress may come through, taking care not to upset Velvet or Nicky, the skittish donkeys.

Six-year-old Bonny sat regally on a brown sheepskin, atop chocolate-brown Velvet. Bowen's dad led her with a rope attached to a halter. Velvet followed Nicky, with Aminya on his solid back, holding a bailer's twine rein. At first she looked petrified, and only gradually relaxed enough to say "I don't like this." However, within a kilometre or two, Aminya was in full voice, recounting the story of Watership Downs to Bonny for at least 20 minutes.

As we picked our way through the rough paddock towards the timbered road reserve, which we were to follow to Bonang, we spied at least six emus grazing. They spied us, and ran for the forest. Two other emu sightings enhanced the day's sense of a holiday. One or two kangaroos bounded on the heels of the emus. We stopped once to stretch our sore thighs and buckled legs – Bo had not cried at all, and we were more than half way. After Velvet shied while she was tied up, Bonny got "jelly-legs" and chose to walk. By then, Bo was asleep, cradled in the arms of the rider.

We were thrilled to emerge near the old Bonang schoolhouse, and left the donkeys in a yard. The girls explored the derelict boys' and girls' toilets and shelter sheds. We called in on one of the last older locals, Phil Prendergast. He spoke of his need to remain independent, even though he must keep moving to prevent his joints seizing up.

At the Bonang store, we happily munched on pasties or chicken legs. A chilly wind was blowing on this side of Honeysuckle Range. We waited till 2:30, hoping to rendezvous with a woman on a horse riding from Goongarah (20 kms towards Orbost from Bonang).

I was a bit anxious when we left, because the route home is challenging. So I left a thumb-nail sketch with the shop-owner, saying "If Kath arrives soon, please show her this map." We also decided to tie blue plastic flutterers on the gate. This wonderful idea caused me a lot of extra energy as I forgot to tie them on the first gates, and had to ride back at a canter. The problem was getting on and off to open and close gates with a saddle-blanket that slips as you leap on. Could've been remedied with a surcingle, which Kath later pointed out.

Cypress was in a lather by the time we caught up with the family again. From there on the journey kept up its adventures: Bonny insisted on walking nearly all the way back. The jack, Nicky, began trotting ahead, and Minya fell into a pile of branches. After that, Ian wrapped the rope around Velvet's neck, and she took off with that incredible lop-sided canter donkeys have. Nicky then became almost impossible to hold. We got home, no injuries, and a great sense of relief. Would Bonny come on another adventure like this?

33

Along the Jingallalla with Bonny and Bo (1989)

*B*onny pulled her gumboots on and trudged up the long hill with mum to catch the pony, and Nicky the donkey who pulls the little cart. This was a special treat for Bonny, a trip to visit her friend Megan, who lived a few kilometres along the road, then up a steep hill. Bonny hid her nervousness. She sensed the quick flight in a horse, and sensitivity to noise or movement. But she was keen to keep up with her sister a little. She ran beside the pony laughing at the donkeys trotting a crooked line behind Nicky, stopping when he stopped to have a poo. Then she ran messages for mum and stepdad, as they looked for harness and bike pump. Then she scurried to throw hay to donkeys so they wouldn't walk away, helped mum to carry harness, and tried not to cry too loudly when she tripped over the feed trough. Finally the sulky shafts were pushed into the keepers.

Bo was placed on the pony in front of mum, and then Bonny ran ahead of them to open the gate for them, singing: Left, left, I left my wife in New Orleans, with 25 bucks and a can of beans…the journey had begun! Bonny sat on the sulky next to her stepdad Ian. He hopped off, and left her with the reins alone…heading for the riverbank uhoh…her mother screeched…and he told Bonny to use the reins…'I don't know how..' she cried. He got back in and took the reins. All settling. Bonny decided to walk for a while, jumping over potholes. Then she agreed to ride behind mum for the last kilometre along the Jingallalla, then the steep hill. Bo got in the sulky with dad. Only one near-miss, when the pony stopped suddenly, and Nicky shied up the bank. Bo sat rockstill.

As we went around the last bend, there were three figures coming down the road … Marg, Megan and little Lauren. We were all smiling mile-wide smiles. Bonny slid off, and Megan got a leg up. Lauren got in the sulky beside a drowsy Bo, who moved over for her. It felt like a royal cavalcade riding into the palace grounds. Bonny worshipped the ground that Megan played on. She joined the children at a picnic table drinking apple juice hooray! Next thing, Nicky came over and tried to drink Bo's juice. Bo scared him off with his outraged "Mine"!

To cut a long story short, Megan was invited to come home with Bonny, and they divided up riding in sulky or on horse. After Nicky was released from the sulky, the girls and Bo towed each other in the royal carriage for as long as they had breath to giggle and pull.

Snug in bed with her friend where sister Aminya usually lies, Bonny offered to sing her sleepy song to Megan. No worries about sleep tonight.

Ribbon

ribbon of Jingallalla unwinds
below me, tall white gums guarding
the singing stones as they hum
to the sky and the birds-
songs without words

Cabanandra

Learning the lesson of mortality- life is flawed, and I cannot make the perfection last forever. There has got to be a break in the pattern.

34

On your bike Nona

Nowadays, as a grandmother living in Canberra, with occasional work as a life-coach, I ride my plucky ebike to my Cafe Poets group, to buy essentials, or to have coffee and write. I just realised this vehicle is as close as I can get to a horse for the over-seventy girl...being in the open air, seeing the wind ruffling the leaves and clouds ruffling, is still vital for clearing my mind of worry and anxiety. My husband knows how rarely I enjoy being in a car, but we still enjoy occasional trips to the ocean and the mountains. We have been fortunate to travel widely across the world with his postings as Research Fellow. Sadly, his health has declined so he is not able to get about on his own.

On one trip to Peru, my son Bo in his teens came with us, and climbed to Macchu Picchu for a life-changing adventure, only to end up in emergency with a heart attack. Later in Australia surgery revealed an unusual heart defect, that had it not been found, could have ended in tragedy. Thank you Incas. Peak experiences can reveal an unexpected deep chasm.

The 2022 summer fire season was horrendous for most of Southeastern Australia, and the weeks of smoke in Canberra meant staying indoors. Now to add to the horror, we were in lock down right across Australia and the world due to a pandemic. I still went beetling down to the local shops. The greatest source of relief and joy is that my eldest daughter went with her two girls to her childhood home. Since schools are closed, this was possibly the best place to be. They sent photos of kangaroos, vegetable gardens, getting firewood and my granddaughter had been enjoying riding a horse across the paddocks.

After the lockdown

Since then, she and her beloved partner have a lovely sustainable farm at Goongerah where they grow organic fruit, poultry and cows with permaculture principles. During Covid lockdown, the girls were doing home schooling there. Now that they are teenagers, the family have moved to Canberra not far from me. The eldest is involved in dance and photography, while the younger sister loves tai kwondo, friends and adventure.

My son Bowen stayed at Cabanandra for a few months with his wife and two little ones. Currently they go down as often as work allows. I feel so deeply appreciative that they enjoy the beauty and wonder of Cabanandra (under the Bowen range from which Bo took his name.) Bo is a landscaper, and his wife Michelle a National Park Ranger; clearly wellmatched in their love of nature.

Full circle? In a strange way yes. Eliptical maybe. It is also good to have sold small block of land with the rammed earth house to the man known as 'the man from Snowy River', who even in his 80s rode down across the Snowy River to rescue brumbies and train them. Somehow the horse legend continues, though I no longer ride a flesh and blood horse.

Poetry occupies a creative space in my life in Canberra, as convenor of a weekly meeting of Majura poets since 2009, who respond to my prompt word . Each year we produce a chapbook of our selected poems. This has been a joyful long ride through uncharted terrain. Some poets publish, and others just enjoy writing and listening to poetry.

❧ 35 ❧

Enjoy the ride

As long as we can find ways to enjoy ongoing relationship with our loved ones and the natural world, no adversity will stop us from getting back on the horse. Let's enjoy the ride. Trust in the patched sky no matter what happens- -rain or shine.

Or as my Inspire ACT life coaching card says:

if you play your part
with all your heart
you will have and hold
the pot of gold

Bark

draped with graceful stole
on shoulders
slipping to the forest floor
manna gum holds her pose

exposing sunset shades
of pink to mauve
to olive green
on naked white limbs

she sheds
her defences
from the year before
in January to herald
the New Year

promising to let go of
the old
be willing to grow

Fiona's Song

All that matters is we do our best
To prevent humanity from fouling our nest

Co2 and methane are making a mess
Burn up or freeze is anyone's guess

Using renewable sun wind and sea
Makes good sense and remember they're free
No more denial don't do despair
Time now to show our children we care

No more denial
no more hot air

This song was performed by Fiona at several climate change events
from 2004

www.ingramcontent.com/pod-product-compliance
Lightning Source LLC
Chambersburg PA
CBHW040846120626
46547CB00001B/52